Cambridge Reading Club

L

Series ed

The Lahti File

Richard MacAndrew

GRUPO sm

CAMBRIDGE
UNIVERSITY PRESS

PUBLISHED BY THE PRESS SYNDICATE OF THE UNIVERSITY OF CAMBRIDGE
The Pitt Building, Trumpington Street, Cambridge, United Kingdom

CAMBRIDGE UNIVERSITY PRESS
The Edinburgh Building, Cambridge CB2 2RU, UK
40 West 20th Street, New York, NY 10011-4211, USA
477 Williamstown Road, Port Melbourne, VIC 3207, Australia
Ruiz de Alarcón 13, 28014 Madrid, Spain
Dock House, The Waterfront, Cape Town 8001, South Africa

http://www.cambridge.org

First published 2003
First published under Cambridge Reading Club 2004

Printed in Spain by Cayfosa Quebecor

Typeset in 12/15pt Adobe Garamond [CE]

With thanks to Vesa Sumanen, and Esa Roine and his family, whose friendship and hospitality made my stays in Lahti such a pleasure.

Contents

Characters

Ian Munro: a British spy working for British Intelligence.
Naylor: Ian Munro's boss.
Pentti Virolainen: a laboratory worker in Lahti, Finland.
Sirpa Virolainen: Pentti's sister.
Jorma Lappalainen: a businessman and politician.
Riitta Koivisto: an office worker for a bioengineering company.

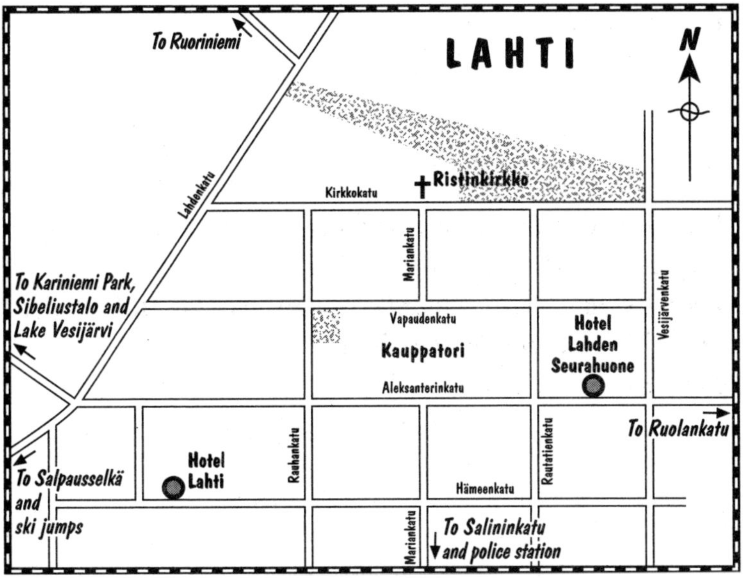
LAHTI
N
To Ruoriniemi
Ristinkirkko
Kirkkokatu
Lahdenkatu
Mariankatu
Vesijärvenkatu
To Kariniemi Park, Sibeliustalo and Lake Vesijärvi
Vapaudenkatu
Kauppatori
Aleksanterinkatu
Hotel Lahden Seurahuone
To Ruolankatu
Rauhankatu
Rautatienkatu
Hotel Lahti
To Salpausselkä and ski jumps
Hämeenkatu
Mariankatu
To Salininkatu and police station

FINLAND
N
Jyväskylä
Lake Päijänne
Vääksy
Lake Vesijärvi
Lahti
Nastola
RUSSIA
Helsinki
Baltic Sea
ESTONIA

FISH DEATHS IN FINLAND

FINNISH POLICE and health workers were yesterday trying to explain the deaths of hundreds of fish in Lake Vesijärvi. The fish were found at the side of the lake, near the town of Lahti, early on Saturday morning.

UPI News – September 3rd

DEADLY GAS ESCAPE KILLS TWO

A FINNISH COUPLE was found dead yesterday in the Ruoriniemi area of the town of Lahti in southern Finland. It is believed that there was an escape of deadly gas from a factory close to the area. Health workers have so far been unable to find out where the gas came from.

Herald – December 21st

Bird numbers down in Finnish town

The Finnish town of Lahti, just north of the capital, Helsinki, has become an almost birdless area. In the spring large numbers of birds usually return to Lahti. This year, however, has been very different. Finnish scientists say that there are already 85% fewer birds than last year in Lahti.

United News Agency – April 14th

Chapter 1 *A job for Munro*

'Read these,' said Naylor, passing three small pieces of newspaper across the table. 'On their own they're not much, but together . . .' He stopped talking and looked out of his office window for a moment, half closing his eyes in thought. 'Together,' he continued, 'they could mean something strange is happening.'

Ian Munro picked up the three short newspaper stories and read them carefully. Some fish were dead and nobody knew why; two people were dead – probably because some poison gas had escaped; and, there weren't as many birds as usual in a town. If they were three stories from three different places, probably no-one would think twice. But they were three stories about the same place, Lahti, in Finland. And they were all stories from within the last eight months. In fact, the last one was dated April 14th, only a few days ago.

Munro looked across at Naylor. Naylor was a tall man with grey hair and hard bright blue eyes. He was dressed in a dark grey suit with a white shirt and a dark blue tie. Munro thought, not for the first time, how little he knew about Naylor. But then Naylor spent his working life sending people on jobs from which they might never return. Perhaps it wasn't surprising that he didn't seem to have a lot of friends.

'I see what you mean,' said Munro, sitting back in his chair. 'What do you think is happening?'

'I'm not sure,' replied Naylor, looking at Munro. 'Poison of some sort. Poison gas, maybe. Possibly someone is making it. But we don't know who or why. Not yet anyway.'

Naylor put the three stories back into the file on his desk. As he closed it, Munro saw the name 'Lahti' written on the front.

'You lived in Finland for some years, didn't you?' said Naylor. 'How's your Finnish?'

'It's fine,' replied Munro. 'People usually think I come from Lapland, north of the Arctic Circle.'

'Good. I want you to go over there. To Lahti.'

Twenty years ago people would have called Ian Munro a spy. Today he was called a 'foreign executive'. It was the same business really, just a different name.

Naylor continued, 'You're on the 12.35 plane to Helsinki, Finland. Your tickets are ready downstairs in the travel office. You've got a meeting in Lahti at six o'clock this evening on the steps of the church in Kirkkokatu.'

'Who am I meeting?' asked Munro.

'A man called Pentti Virolainen. He has some information for us about these stories. Find out what he knows and then wait for my orders. Any questions?'

Munro had lots of questions, but he knew that Naylor would only tell him what he needed to know.

'Just one,' said Munro. 'Why us? I mean it's a Finnish problem. Why don't we let the Finns do something about it?'

Naylor moved forward in his chair and put his hands on the table.

'The information I have at the moment leads me to

believe that it would not be a good idea to tell the Finns what we know. I can't tell you more than that for now. It may become clear later.'

Munro said nothing. Sometimes it made the job easier if you didn't have the complete picture.

Chapter 2 *Meeting at the church*

Seven hours later Munro checked into the Hotel Lahden Seurahuone on Aleksanterinkatu, one of Lahti's main streets. He spoke English to the receptionist behind the desk. He enjoyed speaking Finnish, but it might be an advantage if people didn't know he could. They might give away information, thinking that he did not understand.

In his room he took his clothes out of his suitcase and put them away carefully. He always did this in the same way, so that he would know if someone had searched his room. Munro knew they would find nothing. He never carried important papers. He never carried a gun. If someone found a gun, there were always a lot of questions to answer.

Munro checked his watch. It was already 17.45. Time to go. He looked in the mirror. Light grey eyes looked back at him. His hair, dark brown, almost black, was a bit long, but tidy. He was wearing jeans and a grey top. He picked up his map of Lahti. Just another tourist out sightseeing.

Out on the street Munro checked that no-one was waiting for him. He had already checked at the airport, and when he got off the coach in Lahti. However, it was impossible to be too careful. Last year an executive was killed at Bangkok airport before he had even started the job. There were some very red faces in London that day. The street was busy so Munro took his time checking. No-one was following. Good.

The days were already getting longer. It was still very light, and it was warm for April. As he walked across Kauppatori, the market square, he could see the church rising up over on his right. He knew from some tourist information in the hotel that the church, completed in 1978, was the work of the Finnish architect, Alvar Aalto. Munro usually liked the clean lines that Finnish architects brought to their buildings. He was surprised to discover that the church was rather an ugly building.

Munro turned into the bottom of Mariankatu and started walking up the short hill towards the church. The street was empty. He looked at his watch again. 17.55. There was no-one on the church steps. At the top of the street he looked left and right along Kirkkokatu. A woman was walking her dog, about a hundred metres away to the right. There was an art gallery on the left-hand side of the street. It was closed. Munro crossed the road and stood in the doorway of the art gallery. He could see the church steps, but it would be difficult to see him. The basic condition for a safe meeting with someone you don't know: make sure you can see them before they can see you.

The woman and her dog disappeared round a corner. A boy on a bicycle came along from the left and turned down towards the market square. An old lady in a black dress and black shoes came out of the church, carrying a heavy shopping bag.

18.00. Munro seemed to be looking at the paintings in the window of the art gallery. Something to take back home, perhaps? A present from Lahti. Actually he was checking the streets in all directions and looking up at the church steps again. Where was Virolainen? Minutes passed.

The old lady turned left along Kirkkokatu, crossed the road and went into an apartment building. A cat crossed the road quickly in the other direction and jumped over the low wall round the church grounds. It stopped, sat on the grass and started cleaning itself carefully. Munro looked at his watch although he knew what the time was. 18.10. Still no Virolainen. Five more minutes, then he would go back to the hotel. It would be dangerous to wait any longer. He would call London for new orders.

Just then he heard a noise. The sound of running feet. Munro stepped further back into the doorway. People ran when they were late, but they also ran to get away from danger. A man appeared suddenly from the right-hand side of the church. He stopped at the top of the steps and looked all around him. He looked worried, as if someone was chasing him, but he did not know where they were going to come from next. Munro stayed where he was. If this was Pentti Virolainen, there was a problem. Something was wrong. If someone was chasing Virolainen, Munro shouldn't be here. Above all, this should be a safe meeting. The executive from London should not be put in danger.

Munro heard noise at the bottom of Mariankatu. A car was coming up the hill. The noise seemed loud. Too loud, in fact. Munro looked quickly to his right. Too late he realised what was happening.

Chapter 3 *Waiting for new orders*

The car was a black Mercedes. When Munro saw that there were two men in the front and two in the back, he knew they were not out sightseeing. He got right down onto the ground in the doorway, making himself as small as possible. By the time the car reached the top of the street it was travelling fast, the engine very loud. As it turned the corner into Kirkkokatu, the wheels screamed a little on the road and there were four short sounds. Gun shots.

The Mercedes quickly disappeared down Kirkkokatu, turning right at the bottom into Vesijärvenkatu. Munro looked up from where he was, ready to run across the street. Luckily the men in the Mercedes hadn't seen him. Across the street, Virolainen had not been so lucky. He was lying on his back on the church steps, blood on the front of his shirt. Munro looked up and down the road. There was no-one else around yet. Virolainen was clearly beyond help. Any information had died with him. It was time for Munro to leave.

Back at his hotel, Munro took a whisky from the bar up to his room. His work meant that he saw death more often than many people, but he never got used to it. He drank the whisky slowly and took out his phone. Munro decided a text message was quicker and safer than a phone conversation. Anyway he did not have much to say. Quickly he typed a short message and sent it to Naylor.

MEETING OFF. EXECUTIVE WELL. NEW ORDERS NEEDED.

While he waited for a reply from London, Munro looked through *Etelä Suomen Sanomat*, one of the South Finland newspapers, which he had picked up from the hotel bar. There was a long piece about developments in Finnish bioengineering and an interview with Jorma Lappalainen, a rich businessman who owned a number of bioengineering companies. Lappalainen was saying that Finland should lead the world not just in areas like the Internet and mobile phones, but also in science, and especially bio-engineering. Munro also discovered that Jorma Lappalainen was making a name for himself as an important politician. In fact, the country would soon choose a new president, a new leader for Finland, and Lappalainen was saying that he was interested. The newspaper article ended with some personal information about Lappalainen. He lived with his sister and had homes in Helsinki, Lahti and the south of France. There was also a photo of him speaking to a crowd of people at a meeting in Helsinki. He was a short man with the very fair, almost white, blonde hair that Finnish people sometimes have. He was waving with both hands at the crowd and smiling. A political smile, thought Munro, rather than a smile of truth and happiness. It seemed no more probable that Lappalainen would tell the truth than politicians anywhere else in the world.

A sound came from Munro's phone. He read the message.

WAIT

Munro smiled to himself. Naylor was never a man to use more words than necessary. Anyway, he clearly needed time before deciding the next move. So, how should Munro spend the waiting time?

A few minutes later Munro sat down at a table in the bar and ordered another whisky. While he waited for his drink he looked out of the window at the people walking past on Aleksanterinkatu. Lahti was getting ready for Friday night: young men and women going out to bars and discos to enjoy themselves. He thought back to the time he had spent in Finland: three years as a student at the University of Jyväskylä, followed by a couple of years travelling up and down the country doing all kinds of different jobs. He remembered staying in Lahti for a few months. And he remembered thinking in those days that Lahti seemed to be home to the most beautiful women in Finland. He smiled to himself.

Munro picked up a menu and realised he was very hungry. His last meal had been a long time ago on the plane from Heathrow. As he looked at the menu, he heard a soft voice over his shoulder.

'If you don't understand the menu, perhaps I can help you.'

He turned his head. Looking over his right shoulder were two beautiful dark blue eyes. They were set in a face that was also beautiful: a small but pretty nose, short blonde hair and bright white teeth that were smiling at him at this very minute.

'That would be very kind,' said Munro, smiling back.

'Riitta Koivisto,' said the young woman, holding out her right hand.

Munro took her hand in his and shook it. It felt warm.

'Ian Munro.'

'Are you English?' said Koivisto, taking the menu from Munro and sitting down next to him.

'Scottish,' said Munro, 'but it's an easy mistake to make.'

Koivisto put her head on one side.

'Are you making fun of me?' she asked.

'No,' said Munro seriously.

Koivisto smiled again. She was wearing a bright blue jumper and a short black skirt. She opened her bag, took out some cigarettes and offered one to Munro.

'No thanks,' he said. 'And you shouldn't.'

'I know,' she said. 'But I like a lot of things I shouldn't.' She lit her cigarette and smiled at him again.

'So tell me, what's a handsome Scottish man like you doing in a place like Lahti?' she asked.

Munro laughed.

'I'm just on holiday,' he said. 'Enjoying Finland and meeting wonderful Finnish people.'

'Of course we are wonderful,' she said. 'It is because of the wonderful weather we have here.'

And they both laughed.

'So Ian,' she continued, 'what do you do in Scotland . . . or England?'

At that moment the waiter arrived with Munro's drink. She explained the menu to him and then ordered some open sandwiches for him and a *jaloviina*, a type of Finnish brandy, for herself. While she was ordering, Munro sat back in his chair and looked at her. She was very beautiful and she spoke excellent English, but she asked too many questions. Who was she and why did she want to know so much?

Chapter 4 *A dangerous woman?*

At midnight Munro was standing in the shower in his room at the Lahden Seurahuone. He let the hot water run down his body, washing away the troubles of the day.

There was still no message from Naylor. Virolainen's death had stopped one line of information. Naylor would need time to find another.

Munro turned his thoughts to Riitta Koivisto. She seemed to believe his story that he worked for a bank and was in Finland on holiday. She said she worked for a company called Bioratkaisut. She was only an office worker so she didn't really know what the company did. It was something biological, but she didn't know what. She lived in Nastola, seventeen kilometres outside Lahti, and at eleven-thirty she had left to get a taxi home. Without knowing why, Munro did not believe much of what Koivisto had told him.

Munro stepped out of the shower, drying himself on the large white hotel towel. It had been a long day and he felt tired. As he looked in the mirror, there was a soft knocking at the door. Looking through the spy hole in the door, he saw short blonde hair and a bright white smile. He tied his towel round his waist and opened the door. Riitta Koivisto was standing there, a glass of whisky in one hand and a glass of *jaloviina* in the other.

'There were too many people waiting for taxis,' she said, 'so I came back. I thought you might like a bedtime drink.'

She held out the glass of whisky.

Munro took the glass, smiled and stepped back, letting Koivisto walk into the room. She passed very close to him as she came in. Munro shut and locked the door.

Munro drank a little whisky and put his glass on the table next to the television. Koivisto put her glass next to his. Then she walked up to him and put her hands on his shoulders. She pulled him towards her, kissing him full on the lips. His arms went round her, one hand reaching up, his fingers running through her short blonde hair. He kissed her back, hard.

As his lips came away from hers, he said: 'Friday night's always a problem for taxis.'

'Shh!' she said quietly, putting a finger to his lips. 'Don't talk.'

She stepped back a little, freeing herself from Munro. Then she reached behind her neck, pulled her jumper off and let it drop to the floor. She reached forward again, behind Munro's head, her hand pulling him down, towards her. 'Don't say another word,' she whispered.

* * *

Munro woke up suddenly. He felt terrible. His mouth was dry. His eyes hurt. He had a headache. He looked around the room. It was light outside but this was Finland, the land of the midnight sun. Even in April the days were long. What time was it? What had happened? Why did he feel so bad? He got out of bed with difficulty and made his way to the bathroom, trying to find his watch. On the way he stopped and looked round the bedroom. Riitta Koivisto. That's right. He remembered having a drink with her in the bar and he remembered her coming to his room at midnight. They had made love. But then what? There were two empty glasses on the table by the bed. He picked them up and smelled them. They did not smell unusual. He found his watch. It was already midday. He hadn't drunk very much last night so he shouldn't feel as bad as this. Had she given him some drugs to make him sleep? But why would she want him to sleep? He opened the wardrobe. His clothes were in different places. He looked in the drawers. She had searched here too. His suitcase had moved. She had looked in there as well.

He got into the shower and turned the water on. A thirty-second cold shower woke him up completely. He took two aspirin to clear his head, drank about a litre of iced water from the mini-bar and dressed quickly in jeans, a light blue denim shirt and a brown leather jacket. As he was putting his jacket on, his phone made a sound. He had a message.

CALL ON SAFE LINE

Naylor had found a new way into the problem. Munro was back on the job.

Chapter 5 *Being followed*

Mobile phones were useful but Munro didn't like them. Although it was generally considered impossible to listen in to a conversation on a mobile phone, Munro was not so sure. Finland was the home of Nokia. If anyone could listen in to a conversation, the Finns could. Munro just used his mobile for short text messages that other people would not be able to understand. For a safe line, Munro would need something different. Surprisingly, public phone boxes were the safest. He went out of the hotel onto Aleksanterinkatu to find one.

As he walked along the street, he could hear bits of the conversations around him.

'Shot on the church steps.'

'A terrible thing to happen.'

'Are we going to be safe on the streets any longer?'

'Nothing like that has happened before.'

'In the daytime, too.'

'Virolainen. Yes. Such a kind man. My cousin knew him well.'

'This is usually such a safe town.'

'What is happening in the world today?'

The death of Pentti Virolainen had shaken the people of Lahti. It was a small town of only about 95,000 people. Like almost all the small towns of Finland, it was a safe place. Both adults and children could walk or cycle the streets without danger, at almost any hour of the day or night. But today people seemed worried, afraid even. Their safe world had broken into pieces. Munro felt sorry for them.

He found a phone box. Naylor answered at the first ring.

'Give me the complete picture,' said Naylor.

Munro told him about Virolainen's death and then went on: 'I'd like you to check on a woman called Riitta Koivisto.' Munro spelled the name.

'Who's she?' asked Naylor.

'I don't know,' said Munro. 'She says she works for a company called Bioratkaisut and lives in Nastola. I'd be interested to know how much of that is true. She searched my room last night.'

'I see,' said Naylor. 'Describe her.'

'About 170 centimetres tall. Slim. Good-looking. Short blonde hair. Blue eyes. Intelligent, but good at giving the appearance of not being very intelligent.'

'I'll check on her and let you know if I find out anything,' said Naylor.

'Thanks.'

'OK,' Naylor went on. 'We've had some difficulty finding a way back to Virolainen's information. However, I now have an address for you. Ruolankatu 24, Flat 15B.'

Munro repeated the address back to Naylor.

Naylor said nothing for a moment as if searching for the right words. Then he spoke: 'These people are very dangerous, Munro. They've killed one person already. They could kill again. Be careful with this address. It may be our last chance.'

Munro put the phone down, then immediately picked it up again and called the hotel.

'Hotel Lahden Seurahuone,' said a voice.

Munro put the phone down. After a 'safe' call, it was important to make another call immediately. If you didn't, anyone could ring the last number to find out who you had called.

Munro decided that it would be a good time to have a look at the market place. Before he went to the address at Ruolankatu, he needed to be sure he wasn't being followed. This was more important now than ever before. The market would be a good place to find out if there was anyone behind him.

Munro had not even gone a hundred metres when he saw the first: a man in a dark green jacket. When Munro looked at him, the man suddenly found something in a bookshop window of great interest. Getting away from one person should be quite easy, even in a place as small as Lahti. However, there might be more than one person following him.

Within ten minutes, Munro knew there were more. He took his time looking in shop windows, reading restaurant menus, playing the tourist. He did not go straight down to the Kauppatori but decided to walk around the streets, taking his time, enjoying the sunshine. Twenty minutes later he crossed Aleksanterinkatu towards the market. It was Saturday and the market was busy. Munro moved around looking at everything, changing direction, going back the way he had come, making it difficult for his followers to know exactly where he was going. A couple of times he started to leave the market, but then he seemed to see something which made him turn round and go back for another look.

He now realised the size of his problem. First of all, he was in a box of eight: three men in front at any one time, three behind and one on either side. Secondly his followers were not just on foot. At the west side of the Kauppatori was a line of taxis. Munro had walked up to the first taxi, found out that the taxi driver spoke English and asked the way to the Sibeliustalo, the concert hall near Lake Vesijärvi. As he got near the taxi, he saw two cars stop suddenly and at least two of the followers hurry towards them. He thanked the taxi driver and set off on foot towards the Sibeliustalo. As he did so, one of the followers went over to the taxi and started talking to the driver.

On another day, at another time, Munro would have enjoyed the walk to Sibeliustalo. Today his mind was so full of all kinds of thoughts and plans that he almost missed the entrance to Kariniemi Park. Munro had forgotten what the hard Finnish winter did to the countryside. The snow had gone now but much of the land was still a light brown colour. Only in a few places was the bright green of spring starting to show. Munro was pleased he was here now and not a few months ago when the temperatures were often down to -30 °C. Even so, the lake was still frozen after the winter. Munro walked round to the right, along the side of the lake towards the Sibeliustalo and a couple of cafés. The followers came with him, some in front, some behind.

Munro bought a beer and sat at a table in the sunshine looking north to Vääksy. You could go by boat from Lahti to Vääksy, and then to Lake Päijänne, the longest lake in Finland, and finally all the way to Jyväskylä. He drank his beer and thought about the problem. He did not know who was waiting to meet him at Ruolankatu but if anyone followed him there, it was sure to mean death for both him and anyone he might meet. The followers had not killed him yet because they did not know who he was meeting. He needed to get away from them. Quickly.

He made a plan. There was a phone box near the café and he needed Naylor's help. He called London.

Chapter 6 *Hiding*

After calling Naylor, Munro walked back towards the centre of town, past the bus station. The followers were still with him. He could also see one of the cars parked further down the street. When he arrived at the bottom of Aleksanterinkatu, he took a side street off to the right and turned immediately left into Hämeenkatu. He was walking slowly as he came to the front door of the Hotel Lahti, but when he reached it, he stepped inside quickly and shut the door. For the first time in two hours none of the followers could see him. He had to act quickly.

He had visited the Hotel Lahti about ten years before. He was hoping that the inside of the hotel was the same as it was then. It was. There was no real reception desk – the front door led straight into the bar and restaurant. In front of Munro was a lift; to the left some double doors and stairs. There were a few drinkers in the bar but no barperson. Munro turned left and ran up the stairs. He needed to disappear, to find somewhere to hide.

He stopped at the first floor and looked left and right. There was no-one there. Just closed doors. He heard the front door crash open downstairs. Loud voices. Shouting. He ran up more stairs. As he reached the second floor, he looked left and saw a man trying to open the door to a room. It was only about two o'clock in the afternoon, but the man had clearly drunk far too much. In fact, he looked as if he had been up all night. He had very short grey hair, a grey denim jacket and black jeans. He was moving slowly from side to side while trying to put his key in the door.

'Don't move,' the drunk said in Finnish to the door. '*Voi, perkele*! Stop moving while I put the key in you, you stupid door.'

Munro ran up to him and took the key out of his hand.

'Let me help,' he said.

He could hear the sound of someone running up the stairs. There was no time to lose.

Munro opened the door quickly and pulled the man into the room behind him. He closed the door quietly and looked round the room. On the right was a door to the bathroom; on the left a wardrobe. There were two single beds, a table with a television on it, an armchair and a couple of other chairs. Beside one of the beds was a small table with a half empty bottle of whisky on it.

The grey man moved slowly from side to side, looking at Munro as if he was trying to decide if he knew him or not. Munro thought quickly. He turned the television on and pulled the armchair round in front of it.

'Sit down,' he said. 'Watch this. I'll get you a drink.'

The grey man fell into the chair.

'Room service,' the man said quietly to himself. 'Great room service here.' His head fell forward and his eyes closed.

Munro put his ear to the door to try and hear what was happening outside. He heard a knock on one of the other bedroom doors. He heard the door open and the question:

'Have you seen a man in a brown leather jacket and blue jeans?'

He couldn't hear the answer.

He heard another knock. This time there was no answer. Then he heard the sound of keys. Oh no! They'd got the keys. They were going to search all the rooms. He turned and opened the wardrobe. Inside there were some clothes and a sports bag.

Munro heard the door to the next room open and the voices of the men looking for him.

'He's not in here. You try that one and I'll try over here. We'll search every room if we have to.'

Quickly Munro took off his shoes, his jacket, his shirt and his jeans. He put them in the sports bag and closed it. He took the whisky bottle and put some whisky on his hands, chest and in his hair. He ran his fingers through his hair to make it untidy. There was a black T-shirt lying over the back of one of the chairs. Munro pulled it on.

There was a knock at the door.

'Anyone in there?' a voice said.

The grey man continued sleeping.

Munro lay on the bed wearing only pants and socks and the black T-shirt. His head was turned away from the door, the almost empty whisky bottle close to his face.

He heard the key in the lock.

The door opened and a man walked into the room. He was short with dark hair. He saw the two men: the grey man asleep in front of the TV and Munro 'asleep' on the bed. He went to the first bed and looked under it.

He stood up and looked at the sleeping man on the bed. Munro could not see the man but he felt him move closer to try and look at Munro's face. Then he heard the man make a noise and move back as the smell of the whisky reached his nose.

Munro's heart began to slow down a little, but he knew he was not safe yet. The dark-haired man pushed open the door to the bathroom and looked inside. There was a noise as he pulled back the shower curtain. Munro heard the wardrobe doors open. Please don't look in the bag, he thought.

'Anything in there?' a voice came from outside the room.

Munro heard the man speak: 'No, he's not in here. There's just a couple of all-night drinkers sleeping off the whisky.'

Then Munro heard the wardrobe door close, followed by the door to the room.

Munro waited a few minutes, then turned on his back and looked at his watch. It was almost two-thirty. It would be some time before the followers left the hotel. He lay back on the bed, and thought.

Chapter 7 *Breaking out*

Shortly before four o'clock, Munro got up off the bed. The grey man was still asleep in front of the television. Munro thought that he and the man were probably about the same size. Looking in the wardrobe again he found some old black trousers, and a dark blue wool jacket, also quite old and dirty. In one of the drawers he found a dark blue baseball cap and some sunglasses. Quickly, he changed. Looking in the mirror, he was pleased at the difference.

There were some trainers on the floor so Munro decided to change his shoes too. They were a bit small but not too uncomfortable. Anyway, Munro thought, small trainers would make him walk a little differently. That would be useful. Often we know someone by the way they walk. So it was a good idea to change your walk as well as your clothes. Everything about his appearance was now very different.

As a final touch Munro drank some whisky and put some more whisky over his clothes. Anyone who met him now would think he was in the middle of a weekend he would never remember.

As he moved things from the pockets of his old clothes to his new clothes, Munro turned his phone on and checked for messages. There was just one – from London. It read: VEJ 563.

Before he left the room, Munro looked out of the window down into the car park at the back of the hotel. On the far side was a blue car with a man in the driver's seat. He was smoking a cigarette and reading a newspaper on the wheel in front of him. From time to time he looked up at the back door of the hotel. It was still going to be difficult to get away from the hotel, but at least now they did not know what he looked like.

As Munro went quietly down the stairs, he decided to try getting away through the back door. He was almost sure there would be someone watching both the back and the front. But if there were going to be any problems, the car park at the back was not so public. The London office did not like their executives making trouble in public places.

Munro got to the bottom of the stairs, pushed open the back door of the hotel and half fell into the car park. He wanted anyone watching to think that he had just come from the bar after a few too many drinks. He walked a little way across the car park towards Hämeenkatu, and then he suddenly turned round, moving like a man half asleep, and started walking in the opposite direction. As he did so, he saw the man in the car open the door and start to get out. He was wearing a red T-shirt with the name 'Harri' on it. Perhaps it's his name, thought Munro. Munro looked at him and realised that Harri's orders must be to speak to everyone leaving the hotel. Munro moved closer to the wall of the hotel so that it would more difficult for other people to see them. As Harri came across to Munro, he spoke to him in Finnish.

'Are you having a good party, my friend?' he asked.

'Not bad,' said Munro in Finnish, his voice thick like a man who has had too much to drink.

'I don't drink here much myself,' said Harri. 'I prefer more expensive places.'

‘Got a cigarette?’ asked Munro.

He wanted Harri close to him and he wanted to be sure he didn’t know who Munro was. Harri put his hand into his jacket pocket, but suddenly stopped and looked closely at Munro. Munro couldn’t take a chance. He took one step forward and brought his knee up hard between Harri’s legs. Harri’s head came forward and Munro hit him as hard as he could in the face. This time his head went back and he crashed to the ground. As he did so, however, Munro saw a dangerous-looking knife in Harri’s hand. Munro knew from Harri’s face that he had hurt him and that this fight was now very serious.

Harri got to his feet, his face red with anger. Holding the knife in front of him, he moved towards Munro.

‘You‘ll be sorry for that,’ he said in English.

Munro moved back until he could feel the wall behind him. Harri smiled.

‘You can’t go back any further, my English friend. Now I have you.’

And as he said this, he ran forward. Munro took a step to his right. The knife hit the wall and flew out of Harri’s hand. His hand crashed into the wall and he half fell, turning towards Munro. Munro closed his hand into a fist and threw it hard, crashing it up into the bottom of Harri’s nose. There was a horrible sound as the bone in his nose broke. Harri’s eyes closed. His body dropped to the ground.

Munro looked down at him.

‘I should have told you,’ he said. ‘I’m Scottish, not English.’

Munro’s hand hurt and he was shaking after the fight.

He checked the car park quickly but no-one else was around. He moved the body under one of the cars near the back of the car park and then ran towards Hämeenkatu. Now he had to take care of the men at the front of the hotel.

Chapter 8 *Pentti Virolainen's sister*

Munro ran out onto Hämeenkatu. He looked to the right and, as he expected, there were a couple of men standing and smoking cigarettes outside the front door of the hotel. Quickly Munro looked to the left. Twenty metres away on the other side of the street, facing away from the hotel, was a grey car: number VEJ 563.

Munro turned back to the right. The men had thrown away their cigarettes and were coming towards him.

'Quick!' shouted Munro, in Finnish. 'Call the police. There's a serious fight back there.'

The two men started running towards him. Munro didn't move. The men ran past Munro without looking at him and turned the corner into the car park. It would take them a few seconds to find their friend. Munro did not wait. He ran to the grey car and opened the door. He felt under the seat. The keys were there. Two minutes later he was driving along the road to Helsinki, checking that he really had lost all his followers. When he was sure, he pulled in to the side of the road and sent a short message to London.

THANKS FOR THE CAR

Ruolankatu was a housing development to the southwest of the city centre. Built in the late sixties, there were a number of tall buildings with two or three flats on each floor, set in some pretty woodland. Number 24 was almost at the end of the road and there was a small supermarket on the ground floor.

Munro parked behind the flats and made his way round to the front. He pressed the button by the front door and a voice came out of the speaker next to it.

'Yes? Who is it?' said a woman's voice in Finnish.

'Ian Munro. From London.'

'Come up,' said the voice.

Munro pushed the front door open and climbed the stairs. The door to flat 15B was not open so he knocked quietly on it. For a moment he realised that someone was looking at him through the spy hole and then the door opened, and Munro heard a voice from inside the flat.

'Come in.'

The flat was very small. Munro walked through a short narrow hall into a small sitting room. There was a sofa, an armchair, and shelves along one wall with books, CDs and a CD player on them. There was a door from the sitting room leading into an even smaller kitchen. In fact, the kitchen was more like a cupboard.

Munro turned to look at the woman who had let him in. She was in her mid-thirties, with shoulder-length red hair, blue-green eyes, and a strong, serious face. She wore a shirt that was the same colour as her eyes, white trousers and flat blue and white shoes. She looked tired and worried.

'I'm sorry I didn't come earlier,' Munro explained. 'And I'm sorry about the smell, too. I had a little trouble getting here.'

'That's OK. I'm just pleased you're here,' the woman said in English.

'We can speak Finnish, if you prefer,' said Munro in

Finnish to show that he had no difficulty with the language.

'Thank you. That would be easier,' she said, smiling weakly. 'Would you like some coffee or something to eat?'

Munro realised that he had eaten nothing since he had woken from a drugged sleep at the hands of Riitta Koivisto that morning. It seemed like days ago. He suddenly felt extremely hungry.

'Yes. I'd love something to eat,' he said.

While the woman was in the kitchen, Munro looked round the room. There were books in English and Finnish; the CDs were mainly pop music. There were also family photos – the woman with her parents, a couple of pictures of the parents on their own, and one of a man about the same age as her, perhaps a little older. Munro looked more closely at the photo of the man. It was Pentti Virolainen. The woman looked a little bit like him. They must be brother and sister.

The woman came back into the sitting room with a plate of sandwiches and two cups of coffee. She gave the plate and one of the cups to Munro and then sat down opposite him with the other cup.

Munro spoke: 'Pentti. Was he your brother?'

'Yes,' said the woman. 'How do you know?'

'The pictures.' Munro looked over at the photographs.

The woman put her hands together on her knees and looked straight at Munro.

'Yes, I'm Sirpa Virolainen, Pentti's sister. Just before he went to meet you, he told me everything he knew. I think he realised that something might happen to him. I think he realised that they knew about him.'

Munro reached out and put his hand softly on hers.
'I'm sorry about Pentti,' he said and took his hand away.
'Thank you,' she replied.
'Please,' continued Munro. 'Tell me what he told you.'

Chapter 9 *Answers for Munro*

Sirpa Virolainen looked past Munro through the window behind him, getting her thoughts together.

'You have to understand something about Pentti, you know,' she began. 'He was bright. I mean, he didn't have a great job, he didn't go to university or anything like that . . . but he was intelligent. He did well at school, but he just didn't want to go on studying for the rest of his life.'

Munro sat quietly, watching her, saying nothing.

'Anyway,' she continued, 'he left school at 18 and got a job with a company called Bioratkaisut which had just started . . . '

'Bioratkaisut!' Munro couldn't stop himself speaking.

'Yes. Do you know it?' asked Virolainen.

'I met someone last night who said she worked there.'

'What was her name?' asked Virolainen.

Munro told her but Virolainen shook her head.

'I haven't heard of her,' she said, 'but that doesn't mean she doesn't work there. Pentti and I weren't very close. I mean, we lived in the same town but we didn't see each other very often and we never talked about his work really. Except for the other night.'

'OK,' said Munro. 'Anyway, you were saying . . . '

'Yes. He had a job at Bioratkaisut. He was a laboratory assistant. He helped the scientists with their work. Usually he just organised their equipment. But sometimes he actually helped them with their work.'

She stopped for a moment and drank some of her coffee.

'This woman you met, did she tell you what Bioratkaisut does?' asked Virolainen suddenly.

'Not really,' replied Munro. 'Something biological.'

'Yes that's right,' said Virolainen. 'The company is well known in Finland for its soap and things like that. It also produces a famous cream for keeping mosquitoes away.'

Munro smiled. The mosquitoes could be terrible in the north.

'Well, Pentti began to realise that there was other scientific work going on at Bioratkaisut which was . . . how can I say . . . not in the public interest.'

'I see,' said Munro. 'What sort of work? And how did he find out about it?'

'When he was helping in the laboratory, he could usually understand what the scientists were doing and why. But he realised there were some special areas of work that he was never allowed to help with. At first he thought it was just chance. Then one day one of the scientists left some papers in the laboratory by mistake and Pentti had a look at them.'

Virolainen was speaking more quickly now and her eyes were bright. 'It was work to develop a special kind of poison gas.'

Munro put his coffee on the table. 'Go on,' he said.

Virolainen went on: 'Well, Pentti then kept his eyes and ears open. He thought there were probably only two or three scientists in the company doing this kind of work. They were certainly developing different types of poison gas, but he thought they were working on other poisons as well.'

'And nobody else knew about it,' said Munro.

'No, nobody' said Virolainen. 'And Pentti didn't know who to tell. He didn't think the police would do anything. It would be his word against the word of scientists working for one of the most famous companies in Finland. Then a couple of months ago in Lahti there was a big meeting of biologists from all over the world. By chance Pentti met a British biologist in a bar one evening and . . . well, he didn't tell him everything but he must have told him enough. Last week someone from London phoned him and asked him to meet you.'

Virolainen stood up and went into the kitchen. She opened a cupboard and took out a box of breakfast cereal. She opened the box, put her hand inside and took out a piece of paper. She put the box back, shut the cupboard door and turned to Munro.

'He also gave me this,' she said, passing Munro the piece of paper.

Munro opened the paper and looked at it. Munro was not a scientist, so he had no idea what the writing on the paper meant. However, it was clearly scientific, and probably biological.

'You said that Pentti thought something might happen to him,' said Munro.

'Yes, he thought someone was following him.'

Munro knew the feeling. He looked at the piece of paper again.

'I'd like to keep this,' he said, 'and take it back to London.'

'OK,' said Sirpa.

Munro put the paper carefully in an inside pocket of his blue jacket.

'There is a phone box up the street,' he said. 'I'm just going out to make a call and then we'll decide what to do about you. You can't stay here.'

Munro saw that Virolainen looked less worried than when he had arrived. Some colour had come back into her cheeks. For the first time Munro realised how pretty Sirpa Virolainen was.

Munro got through to Naylor quickly and explained what Virolainen had told him.

'I've got the paper that Pentti Virolainen left with his sister,' he said.

'Good work,' said Naylor. 'I want you to fax a copy to me here as soon as possible.'

'OK,' said Munro, ' but I need to get Virolainen's sister somewhere safe first.'

'Right,' said Naylor.

'I'll take her to Helsinki. It'll take about ninety minutes,' said Munro.

'OK,' said Naylor. 'Make sure she's safe. Fax me the paper. And then call. I've got a lot of information for you and I'll have new orders.'

The line went dead.

One of the things Munro liked about working for Naylor was that he never asked unnecessary questions. If Munro said that Virolainen was not safe, Naylor believed him. If Munro felt Helsinki was the best place to take her, that was fine with Naylor. Naylor had information to give Munro but he would wait until Munro was clear.

Back in the flat Munro explained to Sirpa Virolainen that someone might have followed her brother to her flat.

It was not a safe place any more. He was going to take her to Helsinki because it was easier to hide in the capital.

Ten minutes later they were driving south on the road to Helsinki.

Five minutes after that Munro looked in the mirror. Two large jeeps were driving up fast behind him and he knew that he was in trouble again.

Chapter 10 *Car chase*

Munro's car was probably the only car that Naylor had been able to organise in such a short time. It was not the car that Munro would have chosen. It was not very strong or heavy, nor was it very fast. The jeeps, on the other hand, were strong and fast.

As soon as he saw them, Munro put his foot to the floor, and the car went faster.

Virolainen immediately turned towards him, 'What's the matter?' she asked.

'Look behind us,' said Munro.

Munro was driving at over 160 kilometres an hour but the jeeps were getting closer all the time. He thought quickly. There was no way he could escape by going faster than the jeeps. The motorway was almost empty and they were not near any towns where he might be able to get away in some heavy traffic.

He looked in the mirror. They were still about thirty metres away. Munro looked ahead as far as he could. He had to get off the main road. The only advantage he might have was on smaller roads that were not so straight. He saw a side road coming up on the right-hand side. He let the jeeps come up close behind him then, at the last moment, he pulled the wheel round to the right and turned into the side road.

The first of the jeeps was taken completely by surprise. It continued straight on past the turning. The driver of the second jeep was more awake. He must have seen the turning and realised that Munro might take it. He pulled hard on the wheel of the jeep, taking it up dangerously on two wheels as it went round the corner.

Munro checked the mirror. Only one jeep was left but the driver knew what he was doing. Munro was taking the corners as fast as he could, but the jeep was getting closer again. There were trees along both sides of the road. No turnings at all.

Suddenly they were on a straight piece of road again and the jeep was right behind him. Munro could see the face of the driver in the mirror. Then the jeep hit the back of their car. Munro and Virolainen shot forwards in their seats. The car was thrown across the road and almost off the other side. Virolainen screamed.

'Hold on!' shouted Munro. He could see a forest road further ahead on the left. If he could turn onto that, they might have time to stop the car and make a run for it through the trees. They would never get away in the car, but on foot they might have a chance. The forest road was still fifty metres away and the jeep getting bigger in the mirror.

'Come on! Come on!' shouted Munro to himself. Then to Virolainen: 'When I stop the car, get out and run. I'll follow you.'

The forest road came nearer but so did the jeep. There was another loud crash as the front of the jeep hit the car hard on the left-hand corner at the back. Munro pulled hard at the wheel to try and keep straight but it was no good. Time seemed suddenly to go slow. The car was moving across the road on its side, now on its top, now on its other side. Munro heard Virolainen scream once more as the car turned over again on its way off the road and into the trees.

The thought entered his mind that he must take off his seat belt as soon as the car stopped turning over. But then there was a terrible noise as the car hit the first of the trees, and a loud crash as the car stopped. Munro felt his head hit the side of the car. Darkness came down behind his eyes.

Chapter 11 *In the sauna*

Munro woke up with a terrible headache. He was lying on a wooden seat in a small wooden room. He was in a sauna. His hands were tied behind his back. He turned his head. Lying on the opposite seat, also with her hands tied, was Sirpa Virolainen. Her eyes were closed, her red hair lying across her face. Munro called her name. She moved and opened her eyes, only a little at first, but then wide as she remembered what had happened.

'Where are we?' she asked Munro.

'I don't know,' he answered. He moved about and managed to sit up.

Just then the door opened. A short man with white blonde hair came into the room holding a gun in his right hand. Munro realised that he knew who the man was.

'Mr Munro. Ms Virolainen,' said the man looking at each of them in turn.

'Mr Lappalainen,' said Munro. It was the businessman and politician that Munro had read about at the hotel. Suddenly a number of things became clear, as pieces of the picture fell into place. Lappalainen was interested in bioengineering. Perhaps that interest included poisons too. Also, it might explain why Naylor had not told Munro the complete story. Lappalainen was an important person in Finland. It was difficult to know how many people might take orders from him. It would be easy to talk to the wrong person – someone who was a friend or employee of Lappalainen.

'Ah,' said Lappalainen. 'I see you know who I am.'

'Yes, I do,' said Munro. 'It's difficult not to know one of the most important men in Finland. But I don't know why you've locked us in here.'

'Well, Mr Munro, it seems that you and Ms Virolainen's brother have been putting your nose into areas of my business which are nothing to do with you.'

'Areas of your business?' asked Munro.

'Yes. My business,' replied Lappalainen. Bioratkaisut is one of my companies. I own it.'

Bioratkaisut. That name again. More parts of the picture became clear in Munro's mind.

Lappalainen continued, 'The company does well. It makes a lot of money, not just for me but for Finland.'

'And the poisons?' asked Munro.

'Ah, yes, the poisons,' said Lappalainen. 'Of course developing poisons is not really allowed. But a foreign country – no, Mr Munro, I'm not going to tell you which country – have offered me a lot of money to organise this work. We have developed an extremely strong and cheap poison. They wanted a gas, if possible. Strong, powerful and with almost no smell at all. We have the technology, they have the money. I have to say I'm not quite sure why they want this poison; to start a war maybe, to kill groups of people who do not like their leader. I don't know. To tell you the truth I don't really care. And anyway they offered me so much money that I felt I couldn't really refuse. And of course, I will be able to use the money to become President of my own country.'

'And the scientists?'

'Oh, they get well paid,' explained Lappalainen. 'But they don't really care about the money. You know what scientists are like. They don't care about rules or the law either. They're just interested in science.'

'But, of course, when people find out what has been happening, your chances of becoming President will disappear for ever,' said Munro.

Lappalainen did not look worried.

'Well, I don't know who is going to tell them, Mr Munro, but it certainly won't be you.' Lappalainen took a piece of paper out of his pocket. It was the piece of paper that Sirpa had given him earlier.

'I've got this now,' Lappalainen went on. 'And as you have probably realised you are in a sauna. In Finland we like our saunas very hot, you know, not like in Sweden. Usually we have them between 95° and 100° Celsius. But today I am going to give you a special sauna. A rather hot one. And . . .' Lappalainen stopped speaking and looked from one to the other with a smile on his face. '. . . the terrible thing is that you will find the door impossible to open.' Lappalainen threw back his head and laughed again. Virolainen's mouth opened wide as she realised what Lappalainen was saying. Although it was hot in the sauna, an icy feeling moved up Munro's back.

'So,' finished Lappalainen, 'it is beginning to get nice and warm in here. Goodbye Mr Munro, Ms Virolainen. I don't think you will be telling anyone about my business anymore.'

He turned and left the room. There was a little window in the door. Munro could see Lappalainen through the window checking that the door would not open.

As soon as he had disappeared, Munro spoke: 'Quick! Get over here with your back to me. Let's try and get our hands untied.'

Virolainen sat up and moved across to where Munro was sitting, but it was difficult to reach each other's hands.

The temperature was beginning to rise and Munro could feel the sweat on his face.

'Let's stand up,' said Virolainen. 'It might be easier.'

They stood up, back to back. Munro felt his fingers touch Virolainen's hands. He started to try and untie her but she was tied very tightly. He worked hard but it was no use.

Sweat was now running down his face and he could feel it running down his body inside his shirt.

'Stop!' said Virolainen. 'Let me try to untie yours.'

Munro stopped. He felt Virolainen's fingers working behind him. The temperature continued to rise. Lappalainen had only left ten minutes ago and already Munro felt as if he was burning alive. His shirt was dark with sweat. He could hear Virolainen crying as she pulled and pulled with her fingers.

'I think it's coming,' she said. 'I think I've got it.'

Munro felt her pull once more and then suddenly his hands were free. He quickly turned round to untie Virolainen's hands. Her face was red, her hair was wet with sweat. Munro's hands were shaking, but now that he could see what he was doing he untied her hands in only a few seconds. He turned and threw himself against the door but it didn't move at all. Quickly he started to break off a piece of wood from one of the seats in the sauna.

'Help me,' he said.

Virolainen took hold of the piece of wood too and together they pulled at it. Suddenly there was a crash and it came off in Munro's hand. He turned to the door and using the piece of wood, he hit the small window again and again, trying to break the glass.

Virolainen sat back against the wall unable to do anything.

'Come on! Break!' shouted Munro at the glass.

On about the tenth hit, the glass started to break. Munro hit it harder and harder and finally it broke. Welcome cold air filled the sauna.

Quickly Munro knocked out the broken pieces of glass and put his hand through the window reaching the other side of the door. Saunas don't usually have locks. They don't usually need them. But Lappalainen had put a large and heavy piece of wood against the door to stop it opening. Munro could just reach the wood, but he could not move it. He tried moving it to the left. And then to the right. It still did not move. The sauna started to get warm again as Munro's arm was stopping cold air from coming in through the window. Munro moved his hand as far as he could to the left and then hit the wood as hard as possible. He felt it move. He hit it again. And again. And again. Munro could feel blood running down his hand. Finally there was a crash. The wood fell to the floor and the door shot open. They were free.

Munro carefully put his head outside, looking both ways and expecting trouble. It was Sunday – the factory was empty.

'Let's go,' said Munro, and taking Virolainen's hand he

started running towards some stairs.

'Down,' whispered Munro and they ran down the stairs, trying to be as quiet as possible.

At the bottom of the stairs they looked round. There were some large double doors to the right.

'That looks like the way out,' said Virolainen.

They ran towards the doors.

Munro heard a shot and saw Virolainen fall at the same time. He stopped running and turned back to see how badly she was hit. Quickly he pulled her behind some boxes, looking to see where the shot had come from. He couldn't see Lappalainen anywhere. But he heard his voice.

'I don't know how you are still alive Mr Munro, but you won't be for long.'

Chapter 12 *Fighting for life*

Munro thought from the sound of Lappalainen's voice that he was on the floor above. Virolainen had been hit in the leg. The shot had gone straight through. Munro took out his handkerchief and tied it round her leg. Then he pulled her further behind the boxes.

'Stay here,' he said quietly to her. 'He can't see you from where he is. I'm going to look for him.'

Munro moved around the boxes, keeping his head down and trying to get to the bottom of the stairs. Lappalainen knew that Munro did not have a gun. He would be feeling good about that. But Lappalainen was a businessman and a politician. He was probably not a gunman himself. Guns are dangerous. And Munro knew a lot of different ways of taking guns away from people.

Munro reached the bottom of the stairs and looked up. Lappalainen was not there. Looking along the factory floor Munro saw there were other stairs going up in different parts of the factory. Lappalainen might have come down one of these. He might already be on the ground floor looking for Munro. With his gun.

Munro moved round carefully and quietly. Suddenly he heard a sound behind him. He turned round quickly. Lappalainen was standing there, a gun in his hand. He smiled.

'You have begun to make me rather angry,' he said. 'Now you can show me where you have put Ms Virolainen and then I can send you both on your way.' He waved his gun in the direction of the front of the factory.

Munro turned his back on Lappalainen and started walking. He walked slowly and he could hear Lappalainen following behind him. He wanted Lappalainen to push the gun into his back so that he would know where it was. He walked even more slowly. Lappalainen came right up behind him and Munro felt the hard metal press against him.

Immediately Munro's hand flew up behind his back, knocking the gun upwards. As soon as he hit the gun, Munro started to turn, reaching up with both hands. Lappalainen fired a shot but it went into the air away from Munro. The two men fought. Munro was using both hands to hold the gun and to try and pull it away. Lappalainen was holding on with one hand and using the other to reach for Munro's face and eyes.

Munro realised he was going to have to let go. He was in danger of Lappalainen seriously hurting his eyes. Suddenly Munro let go of the gun, put a hand on each of Lappalainen's shoulders and crashed his head onto Lappalainen's nose. The Finn screamed and the gun fell to the floor. His face was now red and blood was coming from his nose. Munro watched him carefully. Being angry would make Lappalainen stronger, but it would also make him careless. Suddenly he ran at Munro, screaming like an animal and throwing his fists at him. Munro stepped easily to one side and hit him on the side of the head. As Lappalainen went down on the floor, Munro picked up the gun and turned towards him.

Lappalainen was sitting where he had fallen with his

back against one of the boxes. In one hand was a metal bottle. With the other hand he was taking the top off the bottle.

Munro stood and watched him.

'Well, it all seems to be over,' he said, looking up at Munro. 'I don't really like the thought of spending time in prison, you know. And I don't like the thought of not being President either. So it's really quite useful that my company has been so good at making poisons.'

'No!' shouted Munro, but he could do nothing. Lappalainen held up the metal bottle towards Munro and then drank what was inside.

Munro watched as Lappalainen's face changed colour. The Finn reached up to his throat and a strange noise came out of his mouth. Then his body shook once and he stopped moving.

Chapter 13 *An unwelcome phone call*

Munro and Virolainen spent the next day helping the police at the Salininkatu police station. Munro had called Naylor in London and told him what had happened. Naylor had told him not to keep any information back from the police. With Lappalainen now dead, people would be more interested in telling the truth. Teams of police searched the Bioratkaisut factory and all the scientists were brought in for questioning. Radio and television services carried the news of Lappalainen's death saying only that he had had a heart problem. Being a full-time politician and running a busy company at the same time had been too much work for him. The truth was not necessary, and Bioratkaisut would have enough problems when the public found out that it had produced poison gas for a foreign country.

Munro told the police about Riitta Koivisto and another piece of the picture fell into place. Riitta Koivisto was Jorma Lappalainen's sister. Koivisto was her married name, although she was no longer married to her husband. Munro remembered from the newspaper that she lived with her brother. Since she had searched his room at the hotel, it seemed probable that she was involved in her brother's plans too. Lappalainen's homes in Finland and France were immediately searched. But Koivisto had disappeared.

The following day Munro took Virolainen back to her Ruolankatu flat. The hospital had looked at her leg and allowed her to go home but she was not walking very well. As she put the key in the door of her flat and opened it, she turned to Munro.

'Come in Ian,' she said, smiling at him.

As soon as they were inside the flat, she turned to face Munro. Pulling him towards her she reached up and kissed him hard on the lips. As she stepped back, Munro saw that her leg was clearly hurting her. He reached out and putting one arm under her knees and the other round her shoulders, he carried her into the small bedroom and put her down carefully on her feet by the bed. Munro again realised how beautiful this woman was. She pulled him towards her again, kissing him full on the mouth. Her body moved towards his, pressing close against him. She moved back a little and looked at him, running her fingers through his hair. They kissed again more impatiently and Virolainen reached to undo the buttons of Munro's shirt.

'Love me, Ian,' she said quietly, looking straight into his eyes. 'Make love to me.'

* * *

Back at his hotel the next morning, Munro packed his bag and went down to the reception desk to check out. He had promised to go to Ruolankatu to say goodbye to Sirpa Virolainen before catching the coach to Vantaa airport. He paid his bill, picked up his bag and was turning to leave when he heard a voice.

'Mr Munro.'

It was one of the receptionists.

'Yes,' said Munro.

'There's a phone call for you. You can take it on the phone over there.' The man showed Munro the phone at the end of the reception desk.

Munro picked up the phone.

'Hello.'

'Ian Munro,' said the voice at the other end. 'There is someone here who would like to speak to you.'

Another voice came on the line.

'Ian, is that you?'

It was Sirpa Virolainen.

The first voice came back.

'I hope you know whose voice that was.'

'Yes,' said Munro. Thoughts were flying through his mind. He knew whose the first voice was too. It was Riitta Koivisto. Where was she? What was she doing?

Koivisto spoke again: 'Good. Well, Ms Virolainen and I are at the top of the ski jump in the Salpausselkä area of town. You can see a long way from the top here. It's also a long way down. In fact, if you don't get here very quickly, Ms Virolainen is going to find out just how far down it is.'

'What do you want?' said Munro.

'I want you, Ian Munro,' said Koivisto. 'I want you up here now. Don't call the police. Don't come with a gun. Get in the lift and come up to the top. Now.'

The line went dead.

Munro looked at the phone and put it down slowly. The colour had left his cheeks. His face was white.

'Are you all right, Mr Munro?' asked the receptionist. 'Is there anything I can do?'

Munro looked at him. It took a few moments for Munro to realise what the receptionist had said. Then he spoke.

'Yes,' he said, passing his bag to the man. 'Could you look after this for a few hours? I've just discovered there's something I have to do before I leave Lahti.'

Chapter 14 *At the ski jump*

Munro took a taxi to the bottom of the ski jump. There were three ski jumps next to each other at Salpausselkä. The tallest was sometimes used for the world championships and had a lift that went up to the top. At the bottom there was a small shop which sold T-shirts and tickets to the top. Munro paid and went to wait for the lift. It was a Tuesday afternoon in the middle of April. Nobody was around. On the way up Munro tried to organise his thoughts. He didn't know what to expect when he arrived at the top. He had to follow Riitta's instructions but it was clearly going to be difficult and dangerous.

The lift stopped and the doors opened. The room was empty except for Koivisto standing opposite the door, a gun in her hand. She was wearing jeans and a white sweater. She seemed tired, but there was an angry look in her eye.

'Get out!' she said waving the gun at Munro. Munro moved forward and the lift doors closed behind him. There were stairs on the right going up. And there was blood on the stairs.

'On your knees, Munro,' said Koivisto. 'And you can stop worrying about the girl. She's dead already.'

Munro got down onto his left knee. His heart turned cold. He was too late to help Sirpa.

'So you were in this with your brother,' he said. He immediately realised he needed to keep her talking. He needed a chance to take her gun.

'He was everything to me, my brother,' said Koivisto. 'When my husband left me, Jorma looked after me. He made sure I was OK. He made sure my husband paid a lot of money for leaving me. Then Jorma asked me to work for him. I helped him run some of his companies, including Bioratkaisut.'

She was about two metres away in front of Munro. Too far for him to reach the gun safely. She would shoot him before he got to it.

'So you knew what was happening at Bioratkaisut,' said Munro.

'Of course I knew,' said Koivisto angrily. 'He was making lots of money so that he could become President. He really wanted to be the President of Finland. He knew what this country needed. He had great plans. He would have been a great president. But not now. He's dead. My wonderful brother is dead and it's your fault.'

Down on one knee it was impossible for Munro to move forward without Koivisto realising. She did not take her eyes off him for one moment.

'So how did you know who I was so soon after I arrived in Lahti?' asked Munro. He needed more time. Time to think of something. Time to think of a way of getting to the gun or a way of getting Koivisto nearer to him.

'Lahti is a small place,' she said. 'We knew Virolainen had spoken to a British biologist. And we thought the British might send someone to try and find out what was happening. So when a British tourist arrived, and he didn't have a camera with him to take holiday photos, we thought it would be a good idea to keep an eye on him.'

Just two metres away. Two seconds was all he needed.

Two seconds when she wasn't looking at him.

'So why kill Virolainen's sister?' Munro looked to the right at the blood on the stairs. Out of the corner of his eye he could see that that Koivisto was still watching him. She did not look at the stairs or the blood.

'She tried to stop us too. Just like her brother. Just like you. She gave you information about the poisons we were developing. She helped you. And you killed my brother.' The gun moved a little in Koivisto's hand. She was getting ready to kill him.

'So what now?' asked Munro.

There was little left to talk about now. If he was going to do something, he would have to act quickly.

'What now?' repeated Koivisto, smiling unpleasantly 'Now I'm going to . . .'

At that moment a sound came from the room at the top of the stairs. A half-screaming, half-crying sound. The sound of someone hurt extremely badly. Sirpa!

This time Koivisto's head did move. She looked towards the stairs in surprise. It was the chance Munro was waiting for. He threw himself forward, pushing off hard with his right foot, his hands reaching for the gun. His left hand went over the top of the gun, pushing Koivisto backwards, his right hand went under the gun pushing it up in the air.

There was a loud noise as the gun went off. Koivisto fell back against the wall. The gun flew out of her hand and across the floor into the corner of the room. She did not run after it but instead turned towards Munro. If Munro thought the fight was over, he was wrong. Koivisto looked as if she knew how to look after herself. And she was angry.

She moved right, keeping her hands in front of her.

Munro moved with her, keeping a couple of metres away and watching her carefully. Suddenly Koivisto took a step forward with her left leg. Her right leg came round in a wide circle towards Munro's head. He stepped back and Koivisto's foot went past the end of his nose. Taekwondo. She really was dangerous. But Munro knew one or two Taekwondo moves too.

He stepped a little closer to her. She moved back. He moved a little closer again, not speaking, watching her eyes. In her eyes he saw only a fight for life or death. There was no talking now.

He took a step closer again and this time she came at him, as he knew she would have to. Her hands moved fast towards him, her left hand trying to reach his shirt, her right hand going for his eyes. Munro was ready. He quickly moved to his right, turning as he did so. As Koivisto reached out, she fell forward. Munro's right hand shot out, hitting her on the neck just below the ear. There was a sound like a tennis ball hitting a wall and Koivisto fell, her neck broken.

Munro quickly picked up Riitta's gun from the corner of the room and ran up the stairs. The room at the top had large glass walls on three sides. You could see a long way but Munro did not look out. Sirpa Virolainen was lying on her side on the floor. Munro put his fingers to the side of her neck. She was still alive! He took his mobile phone out of his pocket, and rang 112 for the emergency services.

'Quickly! I need a doctor at Salpausselkä. The top of the ski-jump. There's been a shooting.'

He put his phone down on the ground next to Virolainen. There was blood on the front of her blouse high on the left side of her chest. Carefully he undid the blouse and moved it away. There was a small hole where the bullet had gone in. There was one the other side too, where the bullet had come out. That was good. There was some blood from when she had been shot, but there was no blood coming out now. That was good too.

She made a noise. Her eyes moved and opened.

'It's OK, Sirpa,' said Munro gently, taking her hand. 'You're going to be OK.'

'Yes,' said Sirpa. 'You're here now.'

'Don't talk,' said Munro, smiling at her. 'You're going to be fine. The doctor will be here very soon.'

He looked over the glass wall. Over to the right was Lake Vesijärvi, shining in the sunlight. You really could see a long way. Probably halfway to Vääksy, he thought. Spring in Finland – winter finished, the sun out, and Sirpa was alive and was going to live. For the shortest of moments, his job done, Munro felt everything was right with the world.

Cambridge Reading Club – Level 3

Look out for these other titles in the series:

The Beast *by Carolyn Walker*
'I sleep with my eyes open. My ears hear the smallest sound and I wake. You may see something moving in the corner of your eye. If you turn to look, there will be nothing there. But I am following in the darkness behind you.'

Two Lives *by Helen Naylor*
In the small Welsh village of Tredonald, Megan and Huw fall in love. But is their love strong enough to last? Death, their families and the passing years are all against them.

The House by the Sea
by Patricia Aspinall
A married couple, Carl and Linda Anderson, buy a weekend house by the sea. But one weekend, Linda does not arrive at the house and Carl begins to worry. What has happened to her? Who is the taxi driver that follows Carl?

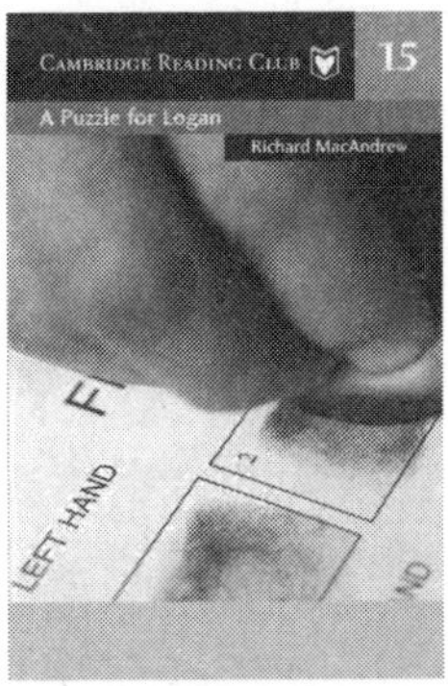

A Puzzle for Logan
by Richard MacAndrew
Inspector Logan has a puzzle to solve: a murderer has escaped from a prison in Scotland and someone has found a young woman's body in a Holyrood Park. Are the events connected?

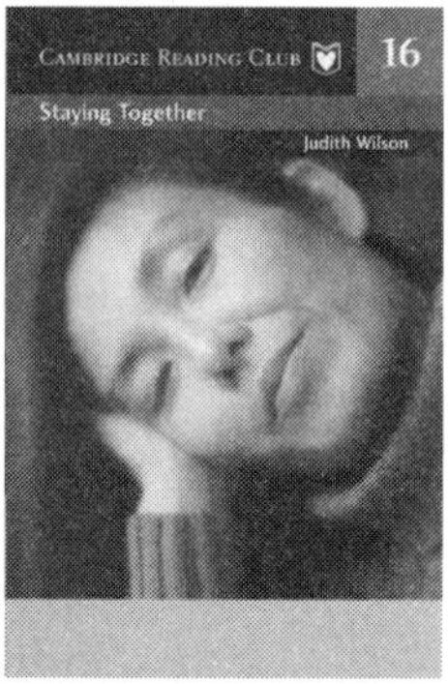

Staying Together *by Judith Wilson*
Ikuko goes to England to study, promising to return to Japan to get married. Ikuko not only discovers another way of life but also a great deal about herself..
This is a powerful story about a love that is carried across three continents.

A Matter of Chance
by David A. Hill
Paul Morris's happy life in Italy changes when his wife dies suddenly. He develops an exciting relationship with Sandra. But all is not as it seems and Paul finds himself involved in a world of international crime.

The Fruitcake Special
by Frank Brennan
Five stories about discovery – a perfume that attracts men, a book that shows people's thoughts, a remarkable change in an old woman's life, the secret of high intelligence, and a way of making time stand still – make up this entertaining collection.

High Life Low Life
by Alan Battersby
Grand Central Station, New York in mid-July. Private investigator Nathan Marley is on his way to another wasted day at the office. But a chance meeting with a homeless woman and a surprise letter changed all of that.